Daya

FLYING HIGH TO SUCCESS, WEIRD AND INTERESTING FACTS ON GRACE MARTINE TANDON!

Learn all about Daya in 20 minutes

With Bern Bolo
The Bathroom Genius

Daya

*

*

*

Flying High to Success

*

*

*

Weird and Interesting Facts on Grace Martine Tandon

By Bern Bolo

TABLE OF CONTENTS

***

INTRODUCTION

Hello, people of planet Earth… we are Martians calling from another planet (*Well… planet Mars of course…*)

We would like to inform you that you are currently under attack. *By us… of course…*

This planet would no longer be yours because it will then be ours – *of course…*

Don't mind the recurring phrase because it's a Martian thing and we like to say it over and over again - *of course…*

Wait… WHAAAT????!!!!

Okay guys, I'm really sorry about that short commercial up there. I just honestly did not know how to open and give a proper introduction to our next topic for this book or e-book, because this talent is just otherworldly and her skills – *oh her voice…*. Her voice is just '*extra-terrestrially*' insane!

Everybody knows her (*even those Martians from the planet Mars – of course… from where else could they be right?*) We could hear her songs even from that forsaken planet. Even aliens love her and WE love her!

Especially the Indian-Americans…

Now, to fully understand what and who the heck am I talking about here because I can clearly picture you out right now with raised eyebrows, scrunched up nose and an overall confused face…

Let me just bring up her name here real quick so you'd have an idea to wipe away that expression from your face…

Okay, you ready?

Okay… our featured artist for this trivia is very well-known for her collab song with The Chainsmokers - the song is *"Don't Let Me Down."*

OH DAYA!!!

Yeah, I heard you…. I heard you just said the exact phrase above. So please LIKE, SHARE, COMMENT or SUBSCRIBE if I guessed that right.

Ooops! sorry… wrong commercial again – thought this was a YouTube video.

Hahahahaha!

But anyway guys… Yes!!!

LET'S GET TO KNOW DAYA!

LET'S GET TO KNOW *DAYA!* (*NOT ZENDAYA AND CERTAINLY NOT*

THAT INDIAN ACTOR...)

So anyway guys, before I started writing about this topic here on my computer...

I did my duty as a writer to do some extensive research about this girl (which is a Standard Operating Procedure...) *of course...*

(Now I'm being a Martian....)

But anyway yes, I did my homework, have piled up some information and details for Daya. But as I went along to the powerful searching tool named '*Google*', I found out that when you type her name in that box called the '*search box*'...

(which was more like of a rectangle than a box, because a box has four equal sides and that one clearly doesn't fit the bill, but anyway, people still consider calling it "the search box" because of course, it'll be a lot awkward if we call it the "rectangular something" or the "rectangular search thingy" or worse – the "rectangular search box" because it would even make that more confusing right? - a rectangular box? Whaaat... That doesn't even make any sense!)

So anyways… as I went and searched Daya's name to gather some details, I found that there are indeed a lot of famous artists similar to her name who Google adds up every time you do the search.

Like the other famous artist - ZENDAYA, which I really thought was DAYA but only with her longer name spelled out and also, there's this actor from India who also turned out to be a "DAYA" too.

So I just want to clear things up here guys that the DAYA I'm talking about here is the one and the only…. **Grace Martine Tandon** which everyone knows by her stage name "DAYA".

So Grace Martine Tandon was born on the 24th of October 1998 to an American slash Indian-American parents. Now, why did I said that? It's because Grace's grandpapa is a native Indian-American Punjabi who is originally from the Punjab province of British India and just transferred to the United States many years ago.

So in the case of Grace's or Daya's ancestors, they are technically called as Punjabi Americans. Her ancestors from his grandfather's side are originally from Pakistan, India or in the South Asia and so Daya is, in short, an Indian-American girl. Even her stage name - Daya is from the Punjabi (*Hindustani to be exact*) native tongue.

Daya means compassion or kindness by the way in Hindustani.

So I know again that I would sound like a broken record with this but - I will repeat that just like other artists I have covered for my trivia's, Daya also has started young with this business. And just like those other artists, she too, loved music even when she couldn't even pull up some floss up in her teeth.

Well… it's not a new thing; it's indeed a singer's thing. They all love music and it's always been their passion.

Well, of course, right?

It would be so damn awkward especially in the interviews when they would be asked if they love their jobs and they would say that they don't because all they need is money and they don't care about the fans and sh*t – right? As for Daya, she started loving music in a very young age. When she was 3 years old, she learned to play lots of instruments like the piano while other little girls at that time were playing Barbie and Ken. And when she was about to reach her teen years, the piano turned to jazz piano along with learning other instruments as well like the guitar, the saxophone and more!

And because she loved music and instruments so much, her parents enrolled her in school for it - the school that will later reshape her destiny in the long run for her passion of music, so when she was eleven, she started going to the Accelerando Music Conservatory which is owned by Christina Chirumbolo and is located in Pittsburgh.

Well, fortunately, Daya or Grace has been extraordinary in this field. She was doing great in the school and a lot of people are turning their heads to her because of her talents and the owner herself has noticed her too. So because of Daya's head-turning talents, Christina, the owner of her then-music school have invited her to meet up with her friend who is the songwriter and producer Gino Barletta. And when they saw Daya's talents (*after her jaw-dropping performance of course*), they invited Daya to Los Angeles to let her work for her career and material.

And oh by the way… both Christina and Gino are also the founders of the music camp named INSIDE ACCESS. So when all of the parties at that time (*Daya and the two producers*) agreed to the said conditions and Daya nodded to working with the INSIDE ACCESS' team, it was like Daya also signed up for her dream's fulfillment as a singer.

And that's just the beginning of Daya's (*not ZENDAYA nor the Indian actor I have talked about, but Daya's*) journey to the world stage!

THE INDIAN-AMERICAN GIRL POP STAR?

So Daya and INSIDE ACCESS really worked well and the singer herself had built quite a connection with Christina and Gino's team. As for Daya, the music camp has totally been a great career-build-up for her and has been definitely a boost to her talents. It has certainly molded her greatly.

Thanks to her parents who accompanied her in this path of her life (*and of course, thanks to mom and dad for driving her all the way to Los Angeles to Christina Chirumbolo's music camp!*)

And since that day, destiny had sealed her fate – she was to become the Hollywood music industry's next big thing! So technically, her professional singing career started at that point in time where she had signed up for INSIDE ACCESS, but since the day was still so young for Daya, her career did not stop there. There were definitely a lot of opportunities piling up. Like really, A LOT...

It was also the time where she had signed up with Paramount Recording Studios and other more music producers. But the most twisting part of this story is the creation of her first ever track, titled "Hide Away".

Ever heard of it?

Oh, it's a very up beating and free-spirited song! Well though mostly it talks about the boys – the good boys most particularly (*if there are still some*) and where the heck are they hiding out, thus the title "hide away."

Part of the song's lyrics says....

"Where do the good boys go to hide away, hide away?
I'm a good, good girl who needs a little company
Looking high and low, someone let me know
Where do the good boys go to hide away, hide away?"

Yeah.., I've actually been asking the same freaking question all this time...

Where do all the good boys go and hide away?!

But anyway, the song is really catchy and as for Daya, surely a lot of teens would get to relate with the song – *and certainly many of us did!*

(*Aherm... I'm only 18, just so you know - I'm 18 before...*) :D

Oh but yes! A lot of people, not only teens loved this song. It's really great and the lyrics could really get your attention. And so, it has become a sensational hit. But did you know that after Daya wrote and recorded this song, she didn't care that much for it and instead she went back to school the next day after recording?

Well, that's true... she did not realize how the song's gonna affect everyone after! It's much of a topic being an LSS (*Last Song Syndrome - you know, the song that keeps repeating in your mind?*) Well this is it. And when talent scout and producer – Zap heard the song and liked it, she called back Daya to finally form a professional and official agreement. So Zap later formed his independent label with Daya's then-first-producer Gino Barletta called the *Artbeatz*.

So you see, everything had been unexpected for our little Indian-American girl at that time. She was only a junior high doing her thing, like friends, exams, proms, boyfriends and more, but as fate would have it – *she became an instant pop star!*

But as always for Daya... *that was still only the beginning...*

THE FIRST BREAKTHROUGH SINGLE: *"HIDE AWAY"*

So yeah… let's discuss this baby…

So we've talked about in the previous pages that this song has truly become Daya's record breaker. It was because of this song she has been discovered and has been signed up to many big record producing companies and labels.

But let's talk more about this "hiding away" shall we?

So okay, Daya have officially released this song as her first single on April of 2015. the song mainly talks about these "good boys" who have gone MIA (Missing In Action) to women. Because you see, the song's message was pretty bold and understandable in any languages, because Daya most certainly has talked about some women who would give everything and strip everything even before their second dates and some women who are just contented with what guys like to offer them – at their convenience. So basically it talks about the women too on how guys should be treating them, not how men should want to treat them. The reason why Daya's constantly asking in the song "Where do the good boys go to hide away", because they are now nowhere to be found…

Or are they???

HAHAHA…

But anyway guys, I'm just telling you about the song's story and background. It is indeed a very good song, but as for our Indian-American artist, success did not show up that fast like your average pizza delivery boy in your doorstep, because it really did take some time before it finally went smooth sailing. She said that it just kept growing over the time passes until it has gotten to where it is now.

And her other songs proved that this girl is not just a one-time-big-time artist because all of her recent songs are also highly praised that even beats up some of the most prominent songs, also most prominent names in the industry these days, like The Weeknd and Adele.

THE WEIRD COLLAB WITH THE AWESOMELY WEIRD EDM DUO THE CHAINSMOKERS FOR *"DON'T LET ME DOWN"*!

And now The Chainsmokers is up with their gimmicks again. But sure we do know that these two are always up to no good, but when it comes to music and their passion, nothing must come to their way into making one, because they're just too good at it. And when they heard about Daya's "Hide Away", these two EDM DJs certainly did not hide away and it was indeed a "perfectly awesome mess" to begin with.

And when the song *"Don't Let Me Down"* was out for fans to listen, everyone just skipped a heartbeat.

I know that too well because I did too...

It was just superb...

So initially, when The Chainsmokers was asked about their collaboration with Daya on the viral song, they would insist that Daya came over to them to help her with the song - but actually no... it was certainly the other way around...

You see, when the media heard about this, they certainly did not believe these two instantly. I mean c'mon! They even say things about their penises, dating hot models and pussies and stuff! And now they would believe this!

Well, if I was them – *OH HELL NO! These guys? Oh, they crazy!!!*

But I am not judging these two with their talents and all; it's just that I just don't want to believe in some of the words coming out of their mouths sometimes anyway.

Well, MOST of the times actually.

LOL.

But yes, it's, in fact, true that Daya did not come to them to make this collaboration because it was them who came to her for the "*Don't Let Me Down*" collab.

And it isn't just me saying that these two are absolutely crazy, because Daya herself thinks so too, saying that these two are weirdos.

But Daya made clear that even though she thinks that way to the duo, well it's only because she thinks of them as her brothers – they tease each other and they do silly things together.

Daya even said that The Chainsmokers are the most real people she's ever met so far in the industry and her collaboration with them for "Don't Let Me Down" was one of the best's things ever happened to her.

Daya claims that the two DJs are the most genuine and she loves both of these weirdos so much because they're great and that they have become a perfect match after the collaboration session with "Don't Let Me Down."

Oh, everything was just weirdly satisfying right? ...

THE INTRODUCTION OF THE FIRST EVER ALBUM

Yes! Of course, this is certainly the part where every artist could bridge each other – the most common thing each of them has… the title of their first official albums!

As for Daya, this is one of the unforgettable moments in her life. *Of course with all that instant fame, who could forget something like this right?*

And truly yes, there were some bumps along the road, but everything still worked within her favor eventually. She went on to make the songs, made some appearances (*because she was already a famed artist at this time – and nothing is a better endorsement than but a pretty face in front of the cam right?*)

So everything has all been set for this first ever album from Daya. And all it needs now is a proper introduction from this book from yours truly…

Hahahaha!

So let me introduce to you Daya's First recorded Album in 2016 – "***Sit Still, Look Pretty***"

Yep… that's all I got. That's the intro….

:D

THE ALBUM: *"SIT STILL, LOOK PRETTY"*

Now I think this album is definitely talking to me…. Isn't it to you?

I think it's telling me……

To sit still, and look pretty!

Well, it literally is right? So please don't give me that look.

But anywho, this is Daya's debut official studio album. It was released by the singer and the labels Z, Artbeatz and RED on October 7, 2016. It has three singles, namely: *"Hide Away", "Sit Still, Look Pretty"* and *"Words"*

And all the tracks on Daya's first Extended Play are included in this project. And they are the following 14 songs:

1. "Dare"
2. "Legendary"
3. "I.C.Y.M.I."
4. "Thirsty"
5. "Love of My Life"
6. "Hide Away"
7. "Cool"
8. "Sit Still, Look Pretty"
9. "Talk"
10. "U12"
11. "Words"
12. "Back to Me"
13. "Got the Feeling"
14. "We Are"

Oh, you'd love these tracks guys – I've listened to each of it - *and now I'm legally insane…*

DAYA CRIED FOR HOURS BECAUSE OF THIS – *FIND OUT WHY...*

Now I'm so glad I got your attention! The title made you look again right?

I know you're very much curious right now about this issue – *why did Daya cried? Did she lost her phone? Forgot to flush the toilet? Missed a lyric? Or failed at lip syncing?*

Whaaatttt!!!!!!!!!!!!!!!

Oh well… she just cried for hours because…….

Well, let's get to know the story first, don't get too excited Daya fan…

So anyway, after this girl had released her successful projects, she then gets to do other cool and very important stuff – and by important, I meant very, very, very important for an also Very Important Person.

Well honestly, that person's not that important actually - I just said that to add some effects to this topic.

So this not-so-very-important-person I am talking about is none other than President Barrack Obama himself…

Oh pshhh… boo hoo! Barrack Obama? THEE BARRACK OBAMA? Well, he's not that important of a person!

Because he is just the president of the United States of America!!!!!!

So anyway, let's keep our cool in place okay?

Yes, Daya made a special number for the family

Wait... Family??? THEE FAMILY!!!!!!!!!

Okay... like I said, "keep your cool." Yes, Daya performed in front of the highest and most prominent families in America. I know it sounds crazy and panicky, right? Don't worry Daya felt that too – actually she felt that so good that it even made her cry and speechless for hours. So the story goes that Daya performed in the Whitehouse in front of the family during the Easter of 2016. And after her performance, the family thanked her of course for her appearance, and that's when she broke down in tears because she said that she was right in front of the President and thats a VERY BIG DEAL!

I mean c'mon! who wouldn't think the same way right?

So Daya said that she did not know what to say, that it just left her speechless and what made her sob is when Michelle Obama actually said that she looked good... that's it... *she...looked... good.*

That then left her sobbing and crying like a hungry baby for hours.

I would even feel the exact same way. He's the president for Pete's sake – she's the president's wife for heaven's sake – I mean, really??? Come the f*ck on, you'd be a total schmuck if you'd say you'd be cool!

I mean imagine this... what would you even say to the President of your country?

"Hey what's up dude, you doin' good and ya'll lookin' fine???" Is that it?

Even if I were in Daya's place... *I'd f*cking cry for days!!!!*

OUR GIRL WINS HER FIRST GRAMMY NOMINATION FOR *"DON'T LET ME DOWN"* AND IT WAS INSANE!

Yay!!! Daya's first Grammy nomination and award!

This is also pretty ridiculously great for our young Indian-American girl. She was only 17 and she won the Grammy's!

That is just insane right!

According to Daya, everything was still surreal for her at that time. She was only a schoolgirl who used to take exams and other fun teen stuff before.

But now, there she was on the stage, in front of all other renowned and notable artists in the music industry holding her first ever recognition in front of the entire world to see. (I am betting that I'd probably pee my pants if that was me) so anyway glad that it was Daya – anyway, she truly deserves it!

"I had just woken up, so I was like 'Is this part of my dream? I can't tell.' And I was so ecstatic I texted all my friends and literally did a lap around my hotel room. I was completely alone but had the energy of like 30 people; it was a moment, for sure. And IT WAS INSANE!"

— Daya

Of course, it was!!! Congrats on the Grammy. :)

REFERENCES

https://en.wikipedia.org/wiki/Daya_(singer)

https://en.wikipedia.org/wiki/Sit_Still,_Look_Pretty_(album)

http://www.billboard.com/artist/6683644/daya/biography

https://short-biography.com/daya.htm

http://www.bbc.co.uk/music/artists/9e8a4e92-1598-47d9-80f7-646802abce76

http://www.harpersbazaar.com/culture/art-books-music/news/a18309/daya-sit-still-look-pretty-interview/

http://www.fuse.tv/2016/09/daya-interview-sit-still-look-pretty-album

http://time.com/4519862/daya-sit-still-look-pretty-interview/

http://www.teenvogue.com/story/daya-interview

http://www.kiddnation.com/backstage-interview-with-daya/

http://people.com/music/daya-the-chainsmokers-weirdos-peoplenow/

http://www.cbsnews.com/videos/daya-interview-on-the-red-carpet/

http://www.billboard.com/articles/news/grammys/7604105/daya-grammy-nomination-reaction-interview-dont-let-me-down

http://www.98pxy.com/media/files/daya-interview-98pxy-summer-jam

http://ktu.iheart.com/articles/ktuphoria-2016-498002/interview-the-chainsmokers-tell-us-how-14781720/

http://abcnewsradioonline.com/music-news/2016/5/5/daya-was-so-happy-she-cried-for-hours-after-michelle-obama-c.html

http://wefoundnewmusic.com/daya-interview/

https://www.instagram.com/daya/?hl=en

https://twitter.com/Daya?ref_src=twsrc%5Egoogle%7Ctwcamp%5Eserp%7Ctwgr%5Eauthor

Check Out Bebe Rexha's Trivia!

The songs, "*Hey Mama*", "*The Monster sang by Rihanna*" and "*Me, Myself and I*", have you heard about them?

Why?......Oh, of course you have… Well, if you're a music geek like me, you wouldn't let pass a very talented singer and songwriter like Bebe Rexha!

Well, this new book is all about her a fun-filled trivia book dedicated just for this girl. She's a "*Bad Bitch*" with "*Sweet Beginnings*" who is just descent enough to "*Fuck Fake Friends*" because she always believed that all she got in this world is her "*Me, Myself and I*" because you see guys we can't blame her… we too, all have "*The Monster*" in every deepest part of us, but just like Bebe Rexha, all we have to do and we must never forget is to still "*Pray*" about it and do everything "*In The Name Of Love*" so there would be "*No Broken Hearts*" for everyone.

See, even almost of her songs fit the bill in our lives. Rexha is indeed one of today's hottest celebrity singers and indeed one of a kind. So don't stop right there and continue to learn more about her. If you're already a fan, then don't just stand there and stare at that computer screen, click on that little button to proceed and check this one out! And also if you have other people to share this with – please don't forget to let them know too and share this entertainment with them as well!

PEACE!!!

Check Out Bebe Rexha's Trivia
[Get your copy of Bebe Rexha's Trivia!](#)

If you enjoyed this "Trivia", please leave an honest review on Amazon.com!

Sign-up here on [Bern Bolo's](#) site for Trivia On Twenty One Pilots!